# WOMEN and the NICARAGUAN REVOLUTION

*Tomás Borge*

**PATHFINDER**
NEW YORK   LONDON   MONTREAL   SYDNEY

Copyright © 1982 by Pathfinder Press
All rights reserved

ISBN 978-0-87348-475-6
Library of Congress Control Number 2009941566

Manufactured in the United States of America

First edition, 1982
Eighth printing, 2018

Tomás Borge was Nicaragua's minister of the interior and a member of the National Directorate of the Sandinista National Liberation Front (FSLN). He was one of the three founding members of the FSLN.

**PATHFINDER**
www.pathfinderpress.com
E-mail: pathfinder@pathfinderpress.com

# CONTENTS

**Introduction**
*Margaret Jayko*     5

**WOMEN AND THE NICARAGUAN REVOLUTION**
*Tomás Borge*     15

*Notes*     41

# Introduction

THE SPEECH BY Commander Tomás Borge reprinted here was delivered in the city of León, Nicaragua, on September 29, 1982, at a rally commemorating the fifth anniversary of the Nicaraguan women's movement. The rally was attended by 2,000 women and men, and thousands more who were unable to enter stood outside. Borge's speech, in keeping with the wide interest in the themes it touched upon, was broadcast live on national radio and reprinted in full in the Managua daily *Barricada*.

This was the first major speech specifically on the question of the status of women by a government leader since the Nicaraguan workers and peasants overthrew the U.S.-backed dictatorship of Anastasio Somoza on July 19, 1979, and established their own government.

In the speech Borge presents a Marxist analysis of the origins, history, and features of women's oppression, explaining why only a socialist revolution, with the full participation of women, could lay the basis for eradicating that oppression. The bulk of the talk is an account of where Nicaragua stands today in this process, and how far it has to go.

Because the talk was given to an audience already familiar with what Nicaragua was like before the 1979 revolution and the big gains that have occurred since then,

Borge did not describe these in any detail. However, it is important for readers in the United States to have a picture of these developments.

For forty-six years, Nicaragua was ruled by the tyranny of the U.S.-installed and U.S.-backed Somoza family. Viewing the country as if it were their personal property the Somozas used their political power to gorge themselves in riches. They owned over 500 corporations and their wealth was estimated at close to half a billion dollars. In contrast, the condition of the majority of Nicaraguans was abysmal.

At the time of the revolution, half the population was illiterate and the figure was much higher in rural areas. The infant mortality rate was 130 per 1,000 live births (nine times higher than in the U.S.) and it was three times higher than that in poorer neighborhoods. Most poor Nicaraguans had no access at all to medical care. Six out of every ten deaths were caused by curable diseases. Only 5 percent of the population had completed elementary school. The unemployment rate was 22 percent and an additional 35 percent were underemployed.

These conditions hit women especially hard. In some rural areas scarcely one woman could read or write. A large percentage of women had to raise families by themselves, thereby bearing the full effects of the brutal living conditions. Those women who were able to find work usually found themselves in the lowest-paying jobs.

Women felt the full effects of government repression as well. Many women involved in the struggle were imprisoned and tortured. Thousands saw their children murdered in cold blood. As one especially brutal way of sowing terror among the population, Somoza's National Guard used rape on a wide scale. There were parts of the country where virtually every woman had been raped by National Guardsmen.

Since 1961, the Sandinista National Liberation Front (FSLN) had waged a many-sided struggle against the Somoza regime. One of the FSLN's goals was the emancipation of Nicaraguan women. The 1969 Sandinista program stated that "The Sandinista people's revolution will abolish the odious discrimination that women have been subjected to . . . it will establish economic, political, and cultural equality between woman and man." Among the specific measures it advocated were creating a nationwide system of day-care centers, granting maternity leave to working women, ending the legal distinction between legitimate and illegitimate children, and eliminating prostitution.

Women played a major role in the struggle against Somoza. During the final stages of the revolution, women made up over 30 percent of the Sandinista fighters. And in working-class communities throughout the country, women played a leading role in the underground organizing activities that led to the revolution's triumph.

After the victory in July 1979, the Sandinistas began to put their program into practice. A literacy drive taught 406,000 people to read and write, reducing the illiteracy rate from 55 to 14 percent. Unemployment was substantially reduced. A massive agrarian reform was carried out; during the first year of the revolution alone, some 45,000 landless laborers gained access to the land. Credit to small farmers increased dramatically.

A concerted effort has been made to bring health care to the entire population. Clinics have been built, and doctors have fanned out into the most remote parts of the countryside. Campaigns to eradicate diseases such as malaria and polio have been successfully completed.

Perhaps the most dramatic change in Nicaragua has been the degree to which the entire population is being drawn into active participation in the decision-making process. Hundreds of thousands of people have joined the numerous mass organizations: the neighborhood Sandinista Defense Committees, the trade unions, the farmers' organizations, the youth organization, the children's organization, the militia, and the women's organization—the Association of Nicaraguan Women "Luisa Amanda Espinoza," named after the first woman member of the FSLN to give her life in the armed struggle against Somoza.

Because of their special oppression under the old regime, Nicaraguan women have benefited especially from all of the changes that the revolution has brought about.

In addition, the Nicaraguan government has made a start in dealing directly with some of the special needs of women. It has started instituting programs such as building production cooperatives, which will also provide jobs for women. Several dozen day-care centers have been set up as a first step in meeting this need as well. The aim in these projects, although they are necessarily limited in scope, is to help draw women into social life.

Steps are also being taken to benefit women workers. The Ministry of Labor has a special project for protecting their health. A new maternity law entitles women workers to forty-five days off both before and after giving birth. The "Statute on the Rights of Nicaraguans," passed shortly after the revolution, lists equal pay for equal work and child care for working women as legal rights. The government has passed a law prohibiting the use of sexist advertising—the practice of using women's bodies to sell different products. Most recently the government has presented a Law on Nurture, one of its chief stipulations being that men have an obligation to share in the upbringing of their children, thus lifting some of the unequal burden that has fallen on the many women who have had to bear this responsibility by themselves.

Especially noteworthy has been the increasing role women are playing in all aspects of the revolutionary process. The Sandinistas see the politicalization of women as indispensable to advancing the revolution, as well as the best guarantee for continued progress toward winning women's full liberation.

As Borge explains, however, there are tremendous challenges that limit Nicaragua's rate of progress in achieving this goal. The major one is the heritage of economic backwardness and dependency that the revolution inherited, a heritage that has also created ideological backwardness in areas such as the status of women.

When the Sandinistas took power the country was totally bankrupt, without foreign currency or foreign savings, and with a debt of $1.6 billion. The civil war caused destruction amounting to more than 35 percent of industrial and 25 percent of agricultural production.

However, these figures tell only a small part of the story. Under Somoza the entire Nicaraguan economy was geared to serving the interests of United States corporations and those of the other major imperialist countries. A sizeable percentage of Nicaraguan property was owned by U.S. businesses. At one point over 90 percent of Nicaragua's exports went to the United States. Nicaragua's status as primarily an agricultural exporter to the capitalist world and an importer of its industrial, technological, and energy resources, kept it in a permanent state of underdevelopment. To make matters worse, an earthquake in 1972 devastated large parts of the country, killing 10,000 people and leaving 200,000 homeless. Most of the damage was never repaired.

This is what the Sandinistas took over. And this underdevelopment can not be eliminated overnight.

Consequently, Nicaragua has felt acutely the effects of the world economic crisis, as have all the other economically dependent countries of Latin America, Africa, and Asia. As the cost of obtaining machinery, spare parts, and oil has soared, Nicaragua's agricultural exports have not been able to keep pace. The result has been a shortage of foreign exchange and growing indebtedness. Unlike countries where the government defends the profit system, however, Nicaragua has not tried to make working people bear the brunt of the crisis. However, these deepgoing economic problems do hold back the progress Nicaragua can make in expanding needed social programs.

An additional challenge has come from the capitalists remaining in Nicaragua. Because the Sandinista government puts the interests of the workers and peasants first, the employer class has lost many of its special privileges. They can no longer hire and fire workers at will nor can they shape the policies of the country to suit their lust for profits. In attempting to create the conditions for the overthrow of the revolution, many capitalists have tried to sabotage the economy, cutting back production and sending their wealth outside of the country, mainly to the United States. This has been the subject of a continual struggle with the Sandinista government.

The most pressing matter Nicaragua faces today is the U.S.-organized war being waged against it. The November 8, 1982, issue of *Newsweek* carried a cover story entitled "America's Secret War—Target: Nicaragua." This article explained how Washington, through the CIA, has organized, armed, trained, and financed an army of thousands of Nicaraguan counterrevolutionaries based in neighboring Honduras, in an attempt to overthrow the revolutionary government. U.S. imperialism is determined to turn back, at all costs, the advance of the socialist revolution in this hemisphere.

Already hundreds of Nicaraguans have been killed by the counterrevolutionaries and the country has suffered millions of dollars' damage. Bridges, roads, crops, and buildings have been special targets of the U.S.-backed forces. In response, Nicaragua has been forced to keep a large part of the population mobilized on a military footing—both men and women—and a large part of the country's material resources have had to go into defense. Tens of thousands of women are participating in the militia and the Sandinista army.

Nicaraguans understand clearly the threat of a full-scale military invasion by Somozaist counterrevolutionaries and the Honduran army, as well as the danger of direct U.S. military intervention—an intervention that would also be directed against the freedom fighters of El Salvador and Guatemala and the revolutionary governments of Cuba and Grenada.

To the extent that the U.S. government is prevented from carrying out its plans, Nicaragua will be able to continue to make progress toward achieving women's liberation as part of building a new society free from exploitation and oppression. The growing sentiment inside the United States against a new Vietnam—which includes opposition to U.S. intervention in Nicaragua—can, if mobilized, play a key role in blocking these war moves.

◆

Tomás Borge's speech will be of particular interest to supporters of women's rights in the United States. It gives a frank description of women's status in Nicaragua, the scope of the challenge ahead, and how to move forward.

Here in the United States there is a new attack on women's rights almost every day: the defeat of the Equal Rights Amendment, continued attacks on abortion rights, challenges to affirmative action—all this despite the fact that the big majority of the population supports these rights. These attacks are being spearheaded by the government. Both Democrats and Republicans have joined in the effort to roll back the gains women have won through years of hard struggle.

Borge's speech shows that unlike in the United States, the government in Nicaragua is pushing forward the struggle for women's rights. The government there is leading, organizing, and educating the population in this fight. It stands squarely on the side of women.

The reason for this is that the Nicaraguan people have eliminated the political domination of the capitalists and have established a government representing the working people and peasants. They are putting the needs of the big majority, rather than the profits of a wealthy few, first. And they have embarked on the road of building a socialist society, where exploitation and oppression will be things of the past.

The Nicaraguan revolution can therefore both inspire and point the way forward for all those involved in the struggle for women's emancipation here and throughout the world.

*Margaret Jayko*
NOVEMBER 1982

# Women and the Nicaraguan revolution

BY TOMÁS BORGE

**COMMANDER TOMÁS BORGE**: How do you feel? Is it too hot in here?

**AMNLAE WOMEN AND GENERAL PUBLIC**: No!

**BORGE**: You're not bothered by the crowded room and by the heat?

**AMNLAE WOMEN**: No! National Directorate, we await your order!

**BORGE**: With all the heat and revolutionary enthusiasm of Nicaraguan women, it's imperialism that should be worried. (Applause and slogans) Because in the hearts of Nicaraguan women there's more than heat—there's fire! (Applause and slogans) I believe that first we should greet the invited compañeras—the compañera representing Venezuela, Minister for Women's Affairs Mercedes Pulido; the compañera representing Cuba, the general secretary of the Federation of Cuban Women [FMC], Dora Carcaño; a group of women representing Chile, Guatemala, and the Dominican Republic; and the ambassador of our sister republic of Bulgaria. (Applause and slogans)

Commander Tomás Borge

Dear compañeras, in the world of today, profound changes are taking place. New offspring of history are being born in the midst of grief, anguish, and heroic splendor. Social revolution is the order of the day in Africa, Asia, and Latin America. Central America is being rocked with social earthquakes. Poor people of all latitudes are demanding—each time more vigorously—profound transformations in the old and rotting structures of class exploitation and imperialist domination.

And in Nicaragua, land of volcanoes and wildcats, we are winning national liberation through the Sandinista revolution.

Therefore it's normal, absolutely logical that we now speak of a new revolution—that is, a revolution of women (applause), a revolution that will complete the process of national liberation.

Many of those women who participate in this revolution live far away from here. Thousands of compañeras couldn't get into this room.

We don't want to make a criticism of anyone, but it seems there was an underestimation of the capacity for struggle and the revolutionary enthusiasm of the masses.

The revolutionary masses have fresh enthusiasm. We couldn't program the presence of 2,000 women here, because something like that cannot be decreed. In fact, thousands of women came who unfortunately could not enter this room.

Let this experience teach us to have more confidence in the masses! (Applause) And above all to understand that our sisters are full of revolutionary spirit and patriotic enthusiasm. (Applause)

We would like to extend a special greeting to the compañera representing the fraternal people of El Salvador, compañera Ana María.

(AMNLAE women shout: "Revolution or death, El Salvador will win!")

At the head of our revolution, I think it would be correct to say, are the mothers of our martyrs, these dear old women we have here in front of our eyes. (Applause)

Inside the revolution, we must understand what should be the position in the social organism of women who forged with their blood the Nicaraguan people. Now it's a question of bringing together the mechanisms that will unleash all the energies and capacities of women so that they become full members of the new society with full rights.

The woman question is nothing more than an aspect of social reality in its totality. The definitive answer to the liberation of women can emerge only with the total resolution of the class contradictions, of the social diseases that originate in a society like ours—politically liberated but with the rope of economic dependence still around our neck.

Nevertheless, we must have patience to deal with the woman question in an independent and concrete manner.

We have to talk about what the position of women was before and after the revolutionary victory, and what the position of women will be in the beautiful future we are going to build. We must also—however briefly—talk about women in the context of the historical development of humanity.

If we read ancient books, we come to know how great the painful discrimination of women has been. In slave society, as in feudal and capitalist society, the working classes were exploited and oppressed.

Women—all women in general—were oppressed, but working women were oppressed and exploited both as workers and as women.

The workers became fully conscious that they were victims of exploitation. Women, too, became conscious of their exploitation as workers but it was a much slower, more complicated process that led them to realize their degree of oppression as women.

Woman was the first enslaved human being on earth. Even before the state of slavery existed, women were slaves.

As you know, dependence and social oppression is based on the economic dependency of the oppressed with respect to the oppressor. Woman was economically dependent on man even before class exploitation arose.

Given this reality, some muddleheaded ideologues have advanced the Philistine sexual philosophy that woman is a dependent being by nature. These ideologues resemble—

as two drops of water resemble each other—those who hold the thesis that the difference between rich and poor always has existed and always will because it falls in the natural order of things.

Experience, however, has demonstrated that relations between the sexes are transformed, like relations between classes, in the process of transforming the means of production and the means of distribution of that which is produced.

Naturally—and this confirms the relationship between sex and the economy in the context of social development, which we don't have time to elaborate on right now—there were epochs when the woman fulfilled the principal role inside the family, under what was called the matriarchy.

But what's important here and what we want to emphasize is that what has predominated is the dominance and the oppression of man over woman.

In ancient times, women completely lacked rights, and today in many places lack rights, and still in Nicaragua women have not won—not even remotely—all their rights. Women were bought for their property just as you buy an object.

Other things were imposed on women, such as strict chastity and a barbaric prohibition of sexual pleasure, while men had the right to live in the same house with several women.

If on their wedding night the man believed or simply suspected that the woman had previously lost her virginity, he had the right not only to repudiate her, but also to kill her. In the past—this was in the past. I should add, although it seems ridiculous, that there still are those who think they have the right to repudiate a woman for these reasons—today, in the present epoch.

According to the fifth book of Moses in the Bible, a man

had the right to repudiate the woman he had recently married even if it was just because she caused him displeasure.

In some societies women were destined to take on the heaviest tasks, treated virtually like draft animals—sometimes with less consideration than a house pet.

Within the family, the birth of a girl was considered a reason for mourning while the birth of a boy was cause for rejoicing and celebrating.

In the Middle Ages there was a certain fashion of romanticism and chivalry toward women, riddled with discrimination as brutal as the use of a chastity belt. Wandering gentlemen left their women in chastity belts and put them in convents for reasons of family honor and many times for economic reasons.

Capitalist society came, under the banner of "equality and brotherhood," to reinforce discrimination against women, fundamentally in the economic arena. The possibility opened, in this stage of development, for women's participation in productive work. The bourgeoisie was interested in enlarging the labor market, so as to have a larger army of unemployed and less pressure for higher wages.

This explains the presence of women in the textile centers, where they began to be exploited as workers and as cheaper manual labor than men.

In modern capitalist society, even when women participate or are allowed to participate in production, there are still strong reminders of the brutal discrimination women suffered in former societies.

Doesn't it really amount to selling a woman, when she marries a rich man without feelings playing any role? What is the act of a landowner or a bourgeois capitalist when he takes a woman worker who is under his domination, under circumstances of nothing more than a self-centered and brutal impulse to possess her, followed immediately by repudiation and repugnance? Isn't a fruit of this inheritance also the masculine pretension that still remains in our underdeveloped countries—countries that have inherited the values of feudal Spain—for the insistence on a woman's virginity at the time of marriage?

The very existence of prostitution—a fact that covers the great cities of the capitalist world—is a direct result of economic discrimination against women, who, to survive and feed their children, are forced to sell their bodies as if they were merchandise.

Today, in the hypocritical world of the bourgeoisie, where the cruel and insulting luxury of the rich exists side by side with the misery, hunger, and nakedness of the dispossessed, women don't just occupy, as I said, a totally secondary place; they are also the object of the most offensive and humiliating exhibitions. They are placed in shop windows so the client can choose which one pleases him the most, as if they were suits of clothes, bottles of whiskey, or slices of ham.

In capitalist society, therefore, bourgeois man gives thanks to the gods, just as the Greek philosopher Plato did, for not having been born a woman, although he also surely thanks God for his ability to insult, sell, exploit, or buy women.

Our people suffered colonial and semicolonial slavery. Slavery gave rise to heroic campaigns of combat in which women not only shared the general suffering of the people and their struggles, but also had to take on the difficult tasks of family reproduction and the constant anguish of knowing that the lives of their children were threatened under the terror of tyranny.

Before the revolutionary triumph, the incorporation of women in productive work was minimal. The great majority of women were condemned to slavery in the home. When women could sell their labor power, in addition to fulfilling their obligations on the job, they had to fulfill their duties in the home to assure the upbringing of their children. All of this in a regime of political oppression and misery imposed by a dependent capitalist society. And subjected, on the other hand, to exploitation by man—the male of the species—who placed on the woman's shoulders the fundamental weight of household chores, thereby endlessly prolonging her working day.

Did this end with the triumph of the Sandinista People's Revolution, we ask ourselves?

The triumph of the Sandinista People's Revolution eliminated terror and opened the way for the process of national liberation, initiating at the same time economic and social transformations that represented a qualitative advance in the conquest of freedom and development.

It can't be said, therefore, that the situation of women in Nicaragua has in no way changed.

The entire society seized its future and women gained the right, taking into account their varied and even spectacular participation in the revolutionary struggle, to participate in an active manner in the process of national transformation.

Nevertheless, all of us have to honestly admit that we haven't confronted the struggle for women's liberation with the same courage and decisiveness.

Independently of the fact that women, in this stage, continue to bear the main responsibility for reproduction and the care of children, the burden of housework and discrimination still relentlessly weighs down upon them.

From the point of view of daily exertion, women remain fundamentally in the same conditions as in the past.

Of course, behind this objective reality there is an economic basis. Workers' living conditions continue to be difficult and incompatible with the political will of the revolution. For reasons that are well-known to you and because barely three years have passed [since the revolution], it has not been possible to meet legitimate expectations for improvement in workers' general living conditions.

This explains why many times women are still compelled to do work that pays no wages, that is not taken account of anywhere, that is not credited toward social security.

Independently of the fact that women often receive the help of men, the truth is that the customs and level of development of our society impose this superexertion on women. And it is in this sense that women are not only exploited—they're superexploited. They are exploited in their workplaces, if they work. They are exploited by lower wages and exploited in the home. That is, they are triply exploited.

What can be done to eliminate this dramatic plight of women?

There is no other alternative except to change the basic economic structure of society. There is no alternative but to develop an economy that guarantees the satisfaction of the fundamental needs of our people. There is no alternative but to create a productive apparatus whose rationale is not individual profit, but rather satisfaction of the demands of the entire society, the demands of the workers—whose rationale is to reaffirm and emphasize the potential of man and woman to live together socially as human beings.

This process of change, compañeras, is complicated, difficult, and will take place over time. But are we going to wait until economic development and social transformation have reached their culmination before we begin to think out the woman question? This would certainly be an inconsistency.

But how can we begin to conceive of women's liberation right now with all the existing limitations?

We took, as we said, the first step, which was national liberation. Now we must take concrete steps to legally guarantee in daily practice full equality between the sexes. (Applause)

Men and women had the right and the duty to fight—to participate in the revolutionary struggle. Women played an outstanding role in the guerrilla struggle, in the clandestine struggle, in self-denial, in sacrifice, and in dedication.

It's no accident that here in León the leaders of the military detachments were women (applause)—among this constellation of women leaders, Dora María Téllez, Vicky Herrera, María Lourdes Jirón, and Ana Isabel Morales[1] are distinguished, among others.

In other parts of the country there were compañeras whose work stood out, even above that of many men—like Mónica Baltodano, Doris Tijerino, Gladys Báez, Olga Avilés, and Eleonora Rocha.[2] (Applause) Women who have certainly continued to distinguish themselves in revolutionary activity.

Right here, on the very soil of León, Luisa Amanda Espinoza shed her blood, and the last guerrilla song of Arlen Siu was heard.[3]

In addition, it was right here that the internationalism of the Mexican compañera Aracelly Pérez ended with the sacrifice of her life alongside the Nicaraguan Idania Fernández. (Applause)

Somewhere in the mountains was stilled the heart of Claudia Chamorro, who had yearned for a child up until the final moment. And today the revolution has made her dreams a reality in the Claudia Chamorro Child Development Center. Claudia Chamorro now has 150 children there—many more than the child she was not able to bear. (Applause)

Women, because of their courage and consciousness, have reclaimed and continue to reclaim their role in Nicaraguan history. Women make up 22 percent of the FSLN. Of all the positions of political leadership in the FSLN, in the regions and provinces, women hold 37 percent. In intermediary leadership positions and the supporting apparatuses, the figure is 24.6 percent. In the Ministry of the Interior, nearly 21 percent of those who work with us are women. (Applause)

At the governmental leadership level, there are a range of compañeras with high-level responsibilities, like Commander Mónica Baltodano and [Minister of Health] Lea Guido. Four compañeras are vice-ministers. Women are also represented in the Supreme Court and in the Council of State.

However, of the fifty-one representatives in the Council of State only seven are women, and women have more right to be represented in the Council of State than simply by the seven they have there. (Applause) This situation is perhaps a reflection of an insufficient participation in the mass organizations present in that body, represented in the Council of State.

On the level of political leadership, there can be no

doubt about the creative participation of compañeras like Dora María Téllez, Vicky Herrera, and Glenda Monterrey [AMNLAE's general secretary], among others.

Today, you learned through the newspapers of the naming of compañera Lea Guido as president of the Pan-American Health Organization. Compañera Lea is the first woman to be named president of this institution in its eighty years of existence. We understand this was done by acclamation, which is an acknowledgment of the important participation of women in our revolutionary process.

In spite of all this—in spite of all the cases mentioned, right now women are not yet massively incorporated into the governmental and political tasks of the revolution.

Let us take a look at a few facts concerning Nicaraguan women. Women workers constitute 40.5 percent of the work force in the country. This means that 183,448 women work outside the home. At first glance, this seems like a very high proportion and could bring us to the conclusion that women's participation in production is very significant. Yet, if we analyze the type of work women carry out, we see that a high percentage of these women are really underemployed, and that another large layer is employed in domestic service—work that is not productive and that will have to be regulated and limited in the future.

What reflects the difficult situation of women is that 83 percent of women who work also carry on their shoulders the weight of economically maintaining their household, raising the children, and doing the household chores. Eighty-three percent—that's barbaric! (Applause)

This indicates to us—in a certain sense—a high degree of family instability and the carefree attitude of irresponsibility many men assume toward a couple's relationship, to say nothing of toward the children. We are all, men and women alike, obligated to be responsible in our love relationships and to be responsible in our family obligations.

The law Glenda [Monterrey] referred to, the Law on Nurture,[4] states that men who father children have to pay their children's upkeep. This is what the Law on Nurture is about! (Applause) As we once said to the women—referring, however, to the men—he who wants to go to heaven will have to pay for it! (Shouts, laughter, applause)

And as for those men who do not comply with the Law on Nurture—the Sandinista Front and the National Directorate will respond in full force, and the Ministry of the Interior is right here to take the necessary measures. (Applause)

I see that the men aren't applauding with much enthusiasm (laughter) and some aren't even applauding (more laughter) and over there I see some who look downright worried. (The audience shouts, "National Directorate, we await your order!") And concerning this there will be no exceptions, no matter who is involved. (Ovation)

How can we fail to seriously consider the equality of

women if we are to be elementally just to their struggle, their sacrifice, and their heroism? How can we not guarantee their participation in social life, in work, and in the political leadership of the country? How can we not guarantee that a woman can be both a mother and a worker, both a mother and a student, both a mother and an artist, both a mother and a political leader, both fulfill all the tasks the revolution demands of her and at the same time fulfill the beautiful work of a self-sacrificing, capable, and loving mother?

A concrete answer to these questions will be possible only to the extent that the individual tasks of women are socialized. It is society that has to provide the necessary day-care centers, laundries, people's restaurants, and other services that will, in effect, free women from household work. This is not easy.

So far, the revolution has only been able to build twenty CDIs [child-care centers]—obviously an insufficient number. The problem is that the cost of construction, equipment, and maintenance is very high. With all the economic difficulties that are holding our country back, it's impossible for us to move forward to the massive creation of these centers. And yet we must do it—not only to enable women to dedicate themselves to productive, social, and cultural tasks, but also to assure that the overall education of our children is as rich as possible.

How can we do it? How can we overcome this contradiction between the possible and the necessary?

We must look for audacious answers, I believe—answers based not so much on purely budgetary considerations but on the initiative, organization, and strength of the masses. Here AMNLAE should be the leading force and catalyst of these initiatives, fundamentally in coordination with the CDSs [Sandinista Defense Committees]. (Applause and slogans)

This is possible in a revolutionary society. There is no task that wouldn't be possible for the revolutionary masses and there is no task that wouldn't be possible for Nicaraguan women. (Applause)

However difficult a task may be, the challenges that are being put forward now can hardly be compared with what Nicaraguan women faced and conquered in the past when they were capable of participating in the trenches with rifles in hand.

On the other hand, the revolution must guarantee equal pay for men and women and at the same time open the doors of production to women's participation in new fields of development—in industry as well as in agriculture.

We have already taken the first steps to guarantee this equal participation. To assure the effectiveness of the principle, "equal pay for equal work," we enacted decrees 573 and 583 for the rural sector. These decrees for the first time established norms governing agricultural labor in coffee and cotton, and provided that everyone above fourteen years of age, man or woman, will be paid directly. Because before the victory, only the head of the household received the wages for the family—the young ones and women were not treated as real workers.

But the important thing is that we watch over the execution of laws the revolution has created to guarantee equality between men and women.

That's why we are going to enthusiastically support AMNLAE's creation of a legal-aid office. We were talking with Doris [Tijerino] a moment ago about the possibility of giving them a lawyer who is a very important cadre in the Ministry of the Interior. If the AMNLAE compañeras accept him, we will gladly offer him to head up this office.

Many women will have to come to this office to lay out their problems, above all after the Law on Nurture takes effect. (Applause)

We are going to redouble our efforts, but to achieve all these objectives, it's essential to involve the entire society. And it's good to emphasize that this struggle will mainly benefit—who? Who will it benefit the most?

(AMNLAE women shout: "The women!")

The women. The men too, but men are full of prejudice and bad habits from the past. Don't pay much attention to us. (Applause. The women shout, "At all costs, we will fulfill our duty to the country!")

At whatever cost we will also fulfill our obligation to women! (Ovation)

Just as workers gained consciousness of the exploitation they suffered and of their vanguard role in the revolution, women must also gain full consciousness of the discrimination they are still subjected to and of their role in the revolutionary struggle. We said that women were triply exploited, which means that women should be revolutionary in three different dimensions, seeking a single objective—the total liberation of our society.

It's good to remember, however, that economic development by itself will not accomplish the liberation of women, nor will simply the organization of women be sufficient.

We have to struggle against the habits, customs, and prejudices of men and women. We have to embark upon a difficult and prolonged ideological struggle—a struggle that equally benefits men and women.

Men must overcome a multitude of prejudices. We know compañeros who are revolutionaries in the street, in their workplaces, in their militia battalions—everywhere—but they're feudal *señores,* feudal lords in the home. (Applause. Borge points to a group of men.) Those men over there say that's exactly right. We've already started something!

These compañeros and all of us inside our homes must—we must—convert ourselves into compañeros of the women, into teachers and students of women—sharing political education with them, sharing in whatever means possible the housework (applause), love and care of the children, and love and defense of the revolution. (Applause)

Equality between men and women shouldn't go in the direction of diminishing respect toward women. Courtesy isn't an attribute of the exploiting classes. Chivalry isn't the private property of the bourgeoisie. We should create a new courtesy and a new revolutionary chivalry—Sandinista courtesy and chivalry of man unto woman. (Applause)

Woman is physically weaker than man, but is as intelligent as man (applause), and from the moral viewpoint—in my personal opinion—is better than man. (Applause) And just as it's the woman who helps us in the difficult hours, we too should offer our support and share not only the happy moments but the difficult ones as well—searching for answers at the time of the most intimate contradictions.

Nor does equality mean lack of gallantry. We have to create Sandinista gallantry (applause), full of good taste, tenderness, and respect toward women; recognizing as well their undeniable merits, their courage in every test, their tenacity and heroism that was demonstrated and continues to be demonstrated in defense of the country.

How could we not raise as a symbol for new generations

of Nicaraguan women the possessor of that famous smile, Brenda Rocha?[5] (Applause)

The constitution of AMNLAE, which was born out of AMPRONAC,[6] is a conquest of women that could only have been produced in a revolution. It's important to remember that the Association of Nicaraguan Women "Luisa Amanda Espinoza" emerged from AMPRONAC in the final stage of the revolutionary armed struggle. Before this, other groups were formed that didn't succeed, for reasons connected with the development of the revolutionary movement, in attracting a great number of women.

Right now, if we consider the path traveled by AMNLAE from the moment of its founding, it's evident that the self-sacrificing activity of the compañeras has achieved quantitative advances, and in some aspects qualitative advances. With respect to the present tasks, and above all regarding the State of Emergency,[7] women's participation has noticeably increased. The work of the Committees of Mothers of Heroes and Martyrs in denouncing the enemy's crimes and plans of aggression against Nicaragua has been outstanding.

However, in the militias, for example, the presence of women varies geographically. In Managua, women are 14 percent of the militia members, but in places like León, their participation is very low. León ranks twelfth in the incorporation of women into the militia, after having been first in the revolutionary struggle in combat against the dictatorship. It's a contradiction that perhaps they will explain to me later.

The participation of women has been important in the People's Health Campaigns.[8] In relation to organizational tasks, we can see a greater stability in leadership cadres, a greater coordination among the various mass organizations, and an advance in the consolidation of the Provincial Executive Committees—and therefore in overseeing the carrying out of tasks in the provinces.

In the field of propaganda, work has advanced to the point of achieving a better definition in the propaganda directed at the rank and file—resulting in better organization.

The planning of campaigns has been more effective—for example around the Continental Meeting of Women[9] and the third anniversary [of the revolution]. The publication of a bulletin was a decisive step toward enriching consciousness about the woman question.

In the field of international relations, it's correct to single out AMNLAE's participation in the Continental Meeting of Women as marking a considerable advance in establishing relations with different political and women's groups worldwide.

It would be an error, however, if we considered these accomplishments satisfactory. The revolution demands that we confront with dedication the deficiencies that limit the development of AMNLAE. The links between the leadership of the association and the ranks are not sufficient. At times general lines of action are put forward without being followed by specific concrete tasks. Adequate forms and mechanisms to assure the active participation of women in the work of the association do not exist.

All this results at times in improvisation and amateurish work habits.

Of course this is not just AMNLAE's problem but a problem of all the mass organizations and forms a part of the process of development of our revolution.

But our revolutionary society has to begin from a fundamental premise—the active, conscious, and permanent participation of each man and woman not only in aspects solely concerned with daily life but also in determining the course of our revolution.

If the masses participate in their workplaces, in their neighborhoods, in their schools, and in their organizations, then this revolution will advance toward a revolutionary society where the dignity of man will be counterposed to the alienation of man.

AMNLAE, for example, should promote the massive participation of women. Events such as the discussion in the Council of State over Patria Potestad [family code] legislation should serve as a source of greater discussion for women in each workplace and neighborhood. This is not to say that men should not discuss this as well, but here we are stressing that AMNLAE should, through massive campaigns, using every available means of communication, promote a discussion among women.

Are women discussing the Law on Nurture?

(AMNLAE leader: "Yes.")

Have you already discussed the Law on Nurture?

(Some AMNLAE women: "Yes.")

All of you?

(The majority of AMNLAE women: "No!")

No, no—not all women. All women must discuss the Law on Nurture and laws dealing with women.

And we must take into account that analyzing this concrete problem means not only gaining knowledge of one particular aspect, such as legislation, but advancing the process of women's politicalization as a whole.

If we don't do this our men and women will not be able to carry the process of liberation to its completion.

Right now AMNLAE should be more a great movement

than an organization—a great movement that encourages the participation of women in the various mass organizations, in the CDSs, in the Sandinista Youth, in the ATC [Rural Workers Association], in the CST [Sandinista Workers Federation]—and that at the same time groups women together in their common bond, which is their status as women.

The central task of AMNLAE should be the integration of all women into the revolution, without distinction. It should be a broad and democratic movement that mobilizes women from the various social sectors, so as to provide a channel for their political, social, economic, and cultural demands and to integrate them as a supporting force in the tasks of the Sandinista People's Revolution.

AMNLAE should become a broad propagandistic, educational, and agitational movement that encourages women to play an active role in the economic, political, and social transformations of the country.

The peasant woman, for example, is a peasant and as such has specific demands. But she is also a woman—just like the woman worker, the woman militia member, the woman who is a housewife, the woman student, the professional woman, and so forth.

Being clear on this dual role is key to the development of AMNLAE.

Another immediate task of AMNLAE, we believe, is to deepen the analysis of the status of the Nicaraguan woman, to fight to massively incorporate women in productive work, to reclaim women's right to participate more fully in production, to participate more fully in leading the government, the mass organizations, and the Sandinista National Liberation Front. (Applause) And to make sure that in scholarship awards, a considerable number are given to women, which in large measure is already happening.

The task of organized women should be—in our opinion—massive involvement, in many different ways, in defense of the revolution. This includes daily defense of the revolution against provocateurs who frequently spread their counterrevolutionary filth in buses, in the supermarkets, and in the streets without getting what they deserve—a dignified and energetic response. We think that women should head up this fight against provocateurs in buses, in supermarkets, and everywhere else. (Applause)

When we see that humble children of our people are continuing to die in defense of the country we know it can't be done any other way.

Barely two days ago in the community of Musawás, fourteen kilometers from Bonanza, there was a new confrontation in which counterrevolutionaries killed four and wounded several others.

From our side, compañero Jaime Sanders, a Sumo Indian from the Atlantic Coast and a member of State Security, fell, in addition to compañeros Jesús Isidro González, Noel Cruz, and Nery Noé García Ruiz—all of whom were from Batallion 80-15 of Masaya and Monimbó.

However, we know how to defend ourselves. Since May we've dealt heavy blows to the enemy, wiping out several counterrevolutionary bands whose only reason for existence was assassination, sabotage, and terrorism.

- In Río Blanco and Bocana de Paiwás, 100 counterrevolutionaries were killed.
- In the Seven Benk region, 90 counterrevolutionaries were killed.
- In Tasbapauni, Bluefields, 6 were killed.
- In Punta Gorda, another 6 counterrevolutionaries.

- A group of 4 involved in the attack on San Francisco del Norte were killed.
- In Moradón, Quilalí, 3 counterrevolutionaries.
- In El Limón valley, 4 counterrevolutionaries from Honduras were killed.

And while we've been talking here, we received a message informing us that near where our four comrades were murdered, 20 more counterrevolutionaries were killed. (Ovation and slogans)

In this same time period, from May to September, we've captured 76 members of the counterrevolutionary bands, which in addition to the number killed gives us a total of 337, plus 20—a total of 357.

Arms of various types have also been recovered, as well as radio transmitters, plastic explosives, freeze-dried food rations—items surely not bought in a supermarket in Tegucigalpa, but delivered by special agencies of the U.S. CIA. We also captured seven pounds of marijuana—which gives us an indication that these people not only carry the arms that imperialism gives them, but also its vices and defects.

Compañeras: We in the Ministry of the Interior have suffered tragic losses for accidental reasons,[10] as you all know. We have decided to bring in a man from the west—and besides being from the west he's from Nicaragua, as he is one of the most distinguished guerrilla commanders, one of the bravest combatants we had during the six or seven years in the mountains: Guerrilla Commander David Blanco, as head of the Ministry of the Interior for this region. (Applause. Women shout: *"Un sólo ejército!"*[11])

Compañeras: Our National Directorate salutes Nicaraguan women with profound respect and affection. We can assure you we are not going to consider anyone a revolutionary who is not ready to fight the oppression of women. (Applause) We would not be Sandinistas if in the new society we did not make women an essential pillar of this new society. (Applause) If we are revolutionaries, even if we are men, we should be with AMNLAE. (Ovation)

From Conchita Alday and Blanca Aráuz[12] to Luisa Amanda Espinoza, women have blazed a path of fire and tenderness that has given life and color to this revolution. Nicaraguan women have not only given the country the fruit of their bellies but also their enthusiasm and courage—selflessly, without limitations.

A revolution with these women is a revolution that will not be defeated by anyone—that will march invincibly into new dawns. (Applause)

It's important that the imperialists know, that the National Guard murderers know, that the nation's traitors know, that in Nicaragua they will be confronted not only by men but by the women as well. (Applause) And these women! Women that leave the fragrance of flowers for the fragrance of gunpowder—women who are as fertile in their wombs as they are in revolutionary consciousness.

Imperialists and members of the bourgeoisie: you will have to confront this sweet rampart of granite. (Applause)

Bourgeoisie and traitors: Here are our women, sisters of Arlen and Claudia and Luisa Amanda, (applause and slogans) here are the sisters of Luisa Amanda standing up in tenderness and heroism, with their hands caressing the delicate skin of their children, with their eyes open and watching, with their fingers on the triggers of their guns and on their lips the war cry of the men and women of this land. Let the Yankee imperialists hear this cry in all its magnitude—this cry that the bourgeoisie should listen to as well—the cry of "Free Homeland . . ."

(The people shout: ". . . or Death!")

(Ovation and slogans)

# NOTES

**1.** Dora María Téllez was one of the leaders of the Sandinista takeover of the National Palace in Managua in 1978, which secured the release of more than fifty political prisoners. Today she holds the rank of guerrilla commander and is political secretary of the FSLN's Managua leadership committee.

Leticia (Vicky) Herrera was a member of the FSLN commando squad that occupied Somozaist José "Chema" Castillo's house in December 1974, securing the release of a number of political prisoners. Today a guerrilla commander, she is national secretary of the Sandinista Defense Committees.

Both María Lourdes Jirón and Ana Isabel Morales were members of the FSLN general staff on the western front during the war against Somoza. Today Jirón works in the FSLN's Department of International Relations and Morales works in the Ministry of the Interior.

**2.** Mónica Baltodano commanded the FSLN forces that took the city of Granada during the 1979 insurrection. Today a guerrilla commander, she is overall coordinator of the FSLN's regional committees.

Doris Tijerino, a longtime leader of the FSLN, is today president of AMNLAE and works in the Ministry of the Interior.

Gladys Báez was a *campesina* when she joined the FSLN in the 1960s. She fought on the western front in the war against Somoza and today is a member of the regional government committee in the León area.

Olga Avilés and Eleonora Rocha participated in the 1974 takeover of the Castillo house and today work in the Ministry of the Interior.

**3.** Luisa Amanda Espinoza was the first woman member of the FSLN to die fighting. She was killed by the National Guard in León in 1970.

Arlen Siu, a student activist in León when she joined the FSLN, was killed by the National Guard in 1975.

**4.** The draft of a law, currently under discussion in the mass organizations, stipulating parental (including divorced, separated, and unmarried fathers) responsibility toward children, as well as children's responsibility toward their parents. Nurture, a social concept in the draft law, includes not just food but also education, shelter, and clothing.

**5.** A fifteen-year-old militia member, Brenda Rocha was the sole survivor of an attack by counterrevolutionaries July 25 in central Zelaya Province. She was seriously wounded in the attack, and her right arm later had to be amputated. A photo of her smiling as she recovered in the hospital has become a national symbol of determination to defend the revolution.

**6.** Association of Women Confronting the National Problem—the "national problem" being understood by everybody to be Somoza. Predecessor of AMNLAE.

**7.** A state of emergency was declared in Nicaragua March 15, 1982, at the beginning of the substantial increase in U.S.-inspired terrorist attacks.

**8.** Preventive health-care campaigns—such as polio vaccination, distribution of malaria pills, and neighborhood cleanups—organized and led by the mass organizations.

**9.** An international peace conference of women leaders from sixty-seven countries, held in Managua on March 24–26, 1982.

**10.** In August, nineteen persons—including a number of State Security personnel—were killed when a military plane crashed after takeoff at Managua airport. Lack of replacement parts, because of the imperialist economic blockade, has resulted in a number of military aircraft accidents in recent months.

**11.** Literally, "One single army!" A slogan heard at virtually every demonstration, it conveys the sense that the entire population is united with the army in defense of the revolution.

**12.** Conchita Alday, fought with Sandino to drive out U.S. Marines.

Blanca Arauz, companion and collaborator of Sandino. Her skill as a telegraph operator facilitated communication among his forces and with supporters abroad.

# FOR FURTHER READING

### Sandinistas Speak
*Tomás Borge, Carlos Fonseca, Daniel Ortega, Others*
The best selection in English of historic documents of the FSLN and speeches and interviews from the opening years of the 1979 revolution. $18

### Nicaragua: The Sandinista People's Revolution
*Tomás Borge, Daniel Ortega, Others*
Speeches, articles, and interviews on the fight against Washington's contra war, the campaign for literacy and education, the fight for equality by the peoples of the Atlantic Coast, and more. $28

### The Rise and Fall of the Nicaraguan Revolution
*Jack Barnes, Larry Seigle, Steve Clark*
Based on ten years of socialist journalism from inside Nicaragua, this issue of *New International* magazine recounts the achievements and worldwide impact of the 1979 Nicaraguan revolution. It traces the political retreat of the Sandinista National Liberation Front leadership that led to the downfall of the workers and farmers government in the closing years of the 1980s. Documents of the Socialist Workers Party. In *New International* no. 9. $16. Also in Spanish.

**WWW.PATHFINDERPRESS.COM**

# The US rulers' political crisis and working people's response

## The Clintons' Anti-Working-Class Record
Why Washington Fears Working People
**Jack Barnes**

Describes the profit-driven course of Democrats and Republicans alike, and the political awakening of workers seeking to understand and resist these assaults.

$10. Also in Spanish, French, and Farsi.

## Are They Rich Because They're Smart?
Class, Privilege, and Learning under Capitalism
**Jack Barnes**

Exposes the self-serving rationalizations by well-paid middle-class layers that their intelligence and schooling equip them to "regulate" workers' lives. Includes "Capitalism, the Working Class, and the Transformation of Learning."

$10. Also in Spanish, French, and Farsi.

## Is Socialist Revolution in the US Possible?
A Necessary Debate among Working People
**Mary-Alice Waters**

An unhesitating "Yes"—that's the answer given here. Possible—but not inevitable. That depends on what working people *do*.

$10. Also in Spanish, French, and Farsi.

**WWW.PATHFINDERPRESS.COM**

# WOMEN'S LIBERATION AND SOCIALISM

## Cosmetics, Fashions, and the Exploitation of Women
#### Joseph Hansen, Evelyn Reed, Mary-Alice Waters

How big business plays on women's second-class status and economic insecurities to market cosmetics and rake in profits. And how the entry of millions of women into the workforce has irreversibly changed relations between women and men—for the better. $15. Also in Spanish and Farsi.

## Women in Cuba: The Making of a Revolution within the Revolution
#### Vilma Espín, Asela de los Santos, Yolanda Ferrer

The integration of women into the ranks and leadership of the Cuban Revolution was inseparably intertwined with the proletarian course of the revolution from the start. This is the story of that revolution and how it transformed the women and men who made it.

$20. Also in Spanish and Greek.

WWW.PATHFINDERPRESS.COM

# Cuba's Socialist Revolution and the World

### Cuba and Angola: The War for Freedom
HARRY VILLEGAS ("POMBO")

The story of Cuba's unparalleled contribution to the fight to free Africa from the scourge of apartheid. And how, in the doing, Cuba's socialist revolution was strengthened. $10. Also in Spanish.

*Companion volume*
### Cuba and Angola
Fighting for Africa's Freedom and Our Own
FIDEL CASTRO, RAÚL CASTRO, NELSON MANDELA, OTHERS

$12. Also in Spanish.

### How Far We Slaves Have Come!
South Africa and Cuba in Today's World
NELSON MANDELA, FIDEL CASTRO

Cuban internationalists "made a contribution to African independence, freedom, and justice, unparalleled for its principles and selfless character," said Nelson Mandela, speaking in Cuba in July 1991 alongside Fidel Castro. Here are their speeches on the victory by Cuban, Angolan, and Namibian combatants over the US-backed South African army that had invaded Angola. $10. Also in Spanish and Farsi.

### Our History Is Still Being Written
The Story of Three Chinese Cuban Generals in the Cuban Revolution

"What was the key measure to uproot discrimination against Chinese and blacks in Cuba? It was the socialist revolution itself." New edition sheds light on Chinese Cubans' involvement in Cuba's internationalist course, including in Africa and Latin America. $17. Also in Spanish, Farsi, and Chinese.

**WWW.PATHFINDERPRESS.COM**

 **PATHFINDER AROUND THE WORLD**

Visit our website for a complete list of titles and to place orders

# www.pathfinderpress.com

PATHFINDER DISTRIBUTORS

**UNITED STATES**
*(and Caribbean, Latin America, and East Asia)*
Pathfinder Books, 306 W. 37th St., 13th Floor
New York, NY 10018

**CANADA**
Pathfinder Books, 7107 St. Denis, Suite 204
Montreal, QC H2S 2S5

**UNITED KINGDOM**
*(and Europe, Africa, Middle East, and South Asia)*
Pathfinder Books, 2nd Floor, 83 Kingsland High St.
Dalston, London E8 2PB

**AUSTRALIA**
*(and Southeast Asia and the Pacific)*
Pathfinder Books, Suite 22, 10 Bridge St.
Granville, NSW 2142

**NEW ZEALAND**
Pathfinder Books, 188a Onehunga Mall Rd., Onehunga, Auckland 1061
Postal address: P.O. Box 13857, Auckland 1643

**Join the Pathfinder Readers Club**
to get 15% discounts on all Pathfinder titles and bigger discounts on special offers.
Sign up at www.pathfinderpress.com or through the distributors above.
$10 a year